Contents

Use this book to find out what you know about Geography. Decide if each statement is

 **True** or **False** before you

turn the page.

There are buildings in
New York that are taller than
Mount Everest.

True or False?

3

The statement on page 3 is **False**

Mount Everest is about 20 times higher than the tallest building in New York.

Mount Everest is 8 848 metres tall.

The Empire State Building is 381 metres tall.

Some mountains are like children. They grow taller every year.

The Himalayas grow six centimetres taller every year.

Six centimetres is about the length of the palm of your hand.

The longest river in the world is in England. It is called the River Avon.

True or False?

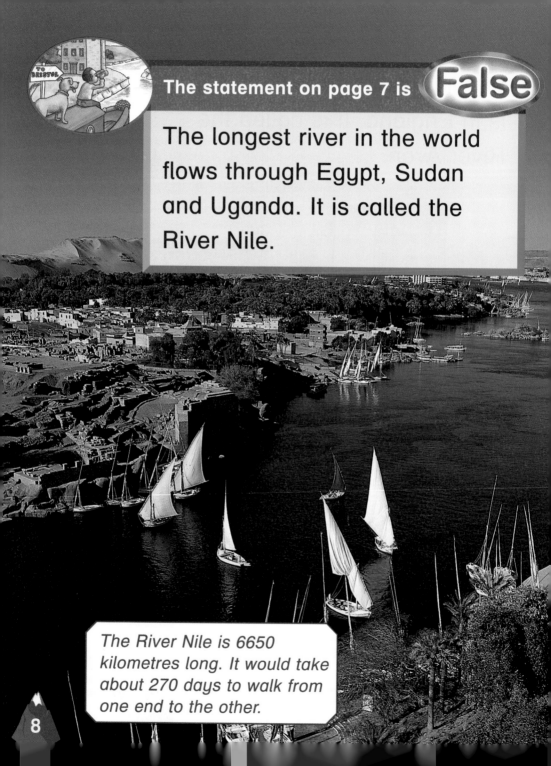

The longest river in the world flows through Egypt, Sudan and Uganda. It is called the River Nile.

The River Nile is 6650 kilometres long. It would take about 270 days to walk from one end to the other.

Icebergs float on top of
the sea.

True or False ?

The biggest part of an iceberg is below the surface of the sea.

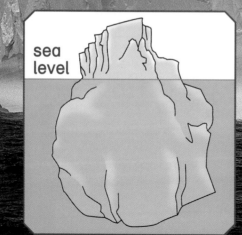

sea level

If the ice at the North Pole melted, the sea would rise and London would be flooded.

True or False?

Some people think that London would be covered by about 30 metres of water. Other places in the United Kingdom would be flooded as well.

North Pole

London

30 metres is as high as two houses, one on top of the other.

It never actually rains
in the Amazon Rainforest.

True or False?

The statement on page 13 is False

Every year, over two metres of rain falls. That is enough rain to cover a grown man.

If you go to New Zealand, you will probably see more sheep than people.

True or False?

The statement on page 15 is **True**

In New Zealand, there are 15 sheep for each person.

Two babies are born in the
United Kingdom every minute.

True or False ?

The statement on page 17 is **True**

At this rate, it takes only three hours to fill an average primary school!

More people speak English as a first language than any other language in the world.

True or False?

More people speak Chinese as a first language than English.

你好吗？

很好，谢谢。

750 million people speak Chinese.

Only 400 million people speak English.

people (millions)

800
700
600
500
400
300
200
100
0

Chinese   English

20

Maps were invented in 1921 by a man called Mark Map when he drew a map of Scotland.

True or False?

The oldest map ever found is over 4000 years old. It shows part of Egypt.

This map was made in 450 BC.

This map was made in 1990 AD.

World map

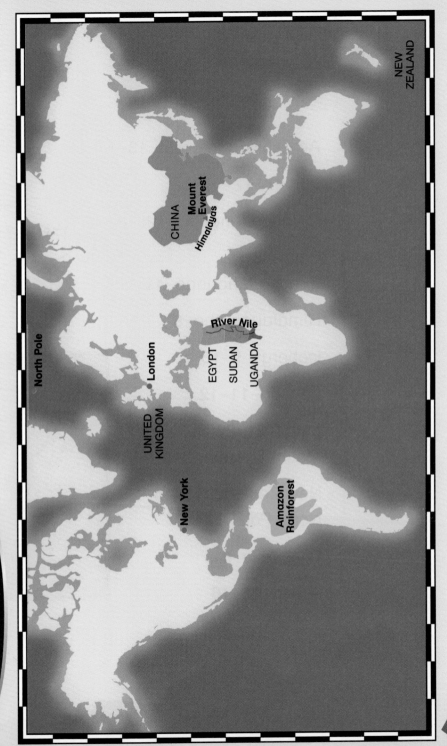

NEW ZEALAND

CHINA

Mount Everest

Himalayas

River Nile

EGYPT

SUDAN

UGANDA

North Pole

London

UNITED KINGDOM

New York

Amazon Rainforest

Index

你好吗？